THE POWER OF FAMILY

Featuring the story of the Trapp Family

Author
Patricia Metten

Art Illustrator
Stephen P. Krause

Editor, Layout and Research
Beatrice W. Friel

THE POWER OF FAMILY

Featuring the story of the Trapp Family

Advisors
Paul and Millie Cheesman
Mark Ray Davis
Rodney L. Mann, Jr.
Roxanne Shallenberger
Dale T. Tingey

Publisher
Steven R. Shallenberger

Director and Correlator
Lael J. Woodbury

AN EAGLE SYSTEMS INTERNATIONAL PUBLICATION
ANTIOCH, CALIFORNIA

Dedicated to families everywhere in the hope that they
will be motivated to strengthen their family spirit.

THE VON TRAPP FAMILY

Maria first joined the von Trapp family when Captain von Trapp appealed to the Reverend Mother at Nonnberg for a governess for his children. The children's mother had died some time before, and it had been difficult finding someone to care for them permanently.

As a graduate of the State Teachers' College for Progressive Education in Vienna and a candidate at the convent, Maria was selected to help out for a period of nine months. However, she fell completely in love with all seven children and their father, and they with her. After consulting with the Reverend Mother, Maria was persuaded by the entire family to marry Captain von Trapp and there followed a very close and beautiful family relationship.

Birthdays and other holidays were always cause for an elaborate celebration in the von Trapp household. Even on ordinary days the children would hurry to finish their homework before supper because they looked forward to spending evenings with the family. Sitting around the fire, the girls would knit or play with their dolls, while the boys would carve wood with their father. Maria would read aloud to them as they busied themselves with their various activities. Afterwards they would sing together. In this manner they enjoyed their long winter evenings. During warmer seasons they often went hiking or on camping trips. As time went on, singing became increasingly more important to them, and they spent many hours practicing.

When political problems in Europe caused their bank to close, it became necessary for them to rent rooms in their home to students attending the Catholic University. After converting one of the rooms into a chapel, there was always a pastor living in their home to conduct Mass in the mornings and benediction in the evenings. One of these priests, Father Wasner, was an accomplished musician and became very interested in the family's singing. With his help the family began a serious study of music and a rigorous practice schedule. Their first public concert was in a competition where they won first place. Although they were offered contracts to give concerts throughout Europe, they were not interested at this time. However, they finally consented to go on one concert tour and met with great success.

The family grew closer as they worked and sang together. Then Hitler's forces invaded Austria, and the family realized that their way of life and their spiritual values were being threatened. Upon holding a family council, they decided that it was worth giving up their material possessions to maintain their way of life. With the pretext of going on a family hiking trip, they packed what few belongings would fit in their rucksacks and fled the country.

Confronted now with the necessity of making a livelihood, they contacted the managers who had previously offered them contracts. "The Trapp Family Singers" were a big hit until people became suspicious of them, thinking they were German spies. Upon being asked to leave one country after another, they finally sailed to America. After their arrival they experienced many hardships, but with constant faith and prayers and much hard work they again found success.

During these years the family increased, as Maria and Georg had two girls and a boy. As time went on, the two older boys served in the service with the mountain ski troops, and the entire family became American citizens.

As the von Trapp family traveled about the country, people were constantly asking them how they could get their own families singing together. This gave the von Trapps the idea to open a family music camp on their property in Vermont. "The Trapp Family Music Camp" was designed to help strengthen family spirit, and the von Trapp family showed their guests how by singing and dancing with them on the lawns and by the brook. The music camp now kept the family busy during the summer months, while the concert tours continued their success during the rest of the year.

Even after Georg had died and the children had married and had families of their own, their family spirit remained close. As the family started to scatter in all different directions, Maria began a new "tradition" which she called family week. This took place the last week in June, when all the family got together for a week of family fun and visiting. The von Trapps found that the only ingredient necessary to be happy, to make others happy, and to strengthen family spirit is love.

I see you holding this book! I'm Nina the Note, a musical note! By the way, do you see me on this page?

"Aha," you think, "this is going to be a story about music!"

That is very good thinking. You're right, but it's also about more than that. It's about a special family that became famous all over the world because of its singing and the success it achieved because of the love and cooperation that each member showed to other family members. Most of all, it's about a very special girl who became the mother of this family and how she helped the family spirit of love and cooperation grow. Her name was Maria.

8

Maria stood in front of the huge door of a house in Salzburg, Austria. Because her hat kept falling down over her eyes, she had to keep pushing it back in order to see. What a big house! Trees, lawns, meadows—the estate seemed to go on forever. Was she dreaming? Was this really to be her home for nine months while she taught Baron von Trapp's seven children? She set her old leather suitcase down on the grass and laid her precious guitar beside it.

The convent she hoped to enter shortly seemed very far away, but she could still hear the words of the Reverend Mother.

"Maria," the Reverend Mother had said, "I hope we have taught you well here. What would you say is the most important lesson we have tried to teach you?"

Maria had answered without hesitation, "Each of us must live the life we were born to live. When God closes a door, somewhere he opens a

window. Each of us must try to understand what is the will of God, and then we must do it."

"That is correct, Maria, and at this moment we believe you must go to the seven motherless children of Baron von Trapp in Salzburg. He came to us to express his great need of a teacher for them and to request our help. Please get your things and leave immediately."

There were not many things to get. Maria had brought with her only the simple, plain clothes she had worn in her native mountain village of Tirol, Austria. And, of course, the guitar, which was never far from her side.

Suddenly the huge door opened.

"Baron von Trapp?" Maria asked of the man who stood there.

"I am the butler," he replied.

Oh dear, a butler! Maria had never in all her nineteen years seen a butler. As she walked into the grand hall of the house, she thought there could not be a more beautiful, elegant place in all the world. She stared at everything.

"Please, do I call him 'Baron von Trapp' or 'Captain von Trapp?' " she asked the butler. Baron von Trapp had been an officer in the Imperial Austrian Navy during World War I.

"Captain," the butler replied, then quietly disappeared.

Coming toward Maria now was a tall, important-looking gentleman. The Captain! He grasped her hand in a friendly manner and then took a whistle from his pocket. After he had made a number of different calls, four girls and two boys solemnly paraded down the stairs. Each one was dressed in

spotless clothes. They each greeted Maria politely but very seriously as the Captain announced their names: Johanna, Martina, Hedwig, Agathe, Rupert, Werner. Soon they marched away as solemnly as they had come.

Then the Captain led Maria upstairs to the bedroom of another little girl, Maria, who was ill at the time and could not get out of bed. She, too, looked at the new teacher with large, solemn, lovely eyes.

Later Maria quickly unpacked her few things. From her bedroom window she beheld a beautiful view of mountains, meadows, trees, and a large park. "What a wonderful place to play games," she thought. She would be back at the convent in a few short months, but in the meantime—oh, those beautiful children! She had fallen in love with them at once. She was determined that while she was their teacher, the time would be filled with fun and laughter, and the lessons would be made as interesting as possible. At home, in her native village, she had loved to climb mountains and to sing and play her guitar. With a group of boys and girls from the Austrian Catholic Youth Movement she had hiked all through the Alps collecting the songs of the people. She knew dozens of them.

17

At the convent her high spirits and joyful nature had made it difficult for her to behave in quite the same way as the others.

"Maria, you must not whistle on the way to chapel."

"I'll try to remember."

"Maria, the banister is to help you climb the stairs, not for sliding down the stairs."

"Please forgive me. I will not forget again."

"Maria, the stones on the courtyard are very slippery, yes. But you must not pretend you are wearing skates and try to slide on them."

"Yes, of course. I won't forget."

"Maria, *skipping* in your convent dress is simply not dignified."

"Oh, yes, of course. I'll remember next time."

And so it went. But here at the Captain's house for these short months, she would find a way to show these children how to laugh and sing. There must be a way!

One day Maria asked the children, "Which tree is your favorite one for climbing?"

"We cannot climb the trees. It would soil our clothes," came the reply.

Maria tried another question: "Where is your volleyball game? You have such a lovely park for games."

"We do not have a volleyball game. In fact, we have no games," they quickly answered.

"Let's go for a hike to the top of that hill beyond the meadow," said Maria eagerly.

"We must not be where we will miss the sound of the dinner bell," was the reply.

What was Maria to do? There must be something they could all do together for the sheer delight of it.

One Saturday afternoon everyone was feeling bored thinking there was nothing to do, because it was pouring a dreary rain outside. Bringing the guitar to Maria, Werner asked, "Do you know how to play it?" Maria answered with a smile, "Yes! Perhaps we could all sing something together." And she began to play and sing.

"We do not know that one," said Hedwig.

"Then we'll try another," said Maria, and she began to sing again.

"We do not know that one either," echoed Rupert.

Maria sang many songs, but none of the children knew any of them. At last she began "Silent Night," and they all joined in. Maria was surprised at how well the children sang together. They really sounded very nice. After "Silent Night" they remembered a few more songs they knew. Maria then sang many of her favorite Austrian folk songs to them, and the time passed so quickly that no one heard the dinner bell!

In this simple, natural way Maria had opened the world of music to the von Trapp children—my world of musical notes.

Maria taught them more songs as time went on. Sometimes the Captain joined the singing or accompanied them on a violin. Before long he began staying home more and making fewer and shorter business trips.

From the first day Maria had seen the von Trapp children, she had fallen in love with them. Then slowly she found herself falling in love with the Captain as well. And the Captain was falling in love with her, too. This was a miracle to Maria, who had planned to return to the convent very soon

now. She sought the Reverend Mother's advice once again to be certain that she was following the will of God for her life. Maria was told that everyone in the convent truly believed it was right that she marry the Captain and become the mother who was so needed in his house.

After Maria joined the family, the life of the von Trapps soon became a song. The family spirit began to change and grow like the melodies the family sang. They all enjoyed being together. The children would even hurry to finish their homework in order to keep their evening free for the activities they loved: knitting, woodwork, reading aloud, and, of course, singing.

The von Trapp family spirit went all out for their birthday celebrations. And with nine people in the family, birthdays came often. Each celebration began the night before with a birthday cake and candles, surrounded by

presents. Each family member waited around the table with a flower until the "birthday child" entered the room and went to each person for a kiss, a birthday wish, and a flower. The presents were then opened by the guest of honor, and he or she became the ruler of all activities for the next twenty-four hours. The next day at lunch there would be more presents, all made by the family, and much hugging and kissing. This type of celebrating was used all year for Christmas celebrations, church festivals, graduations, or any special occasion. The von Trapp family spirit filled these times with laughter, music, fun, and expressions of love for one another.

One day the Captain came to Maria, his face very serious. "Maria," he said, "I have bad news. I have just now received word that our bank has closed. Our money is lost."

However, no one in the family complained about this startling turn of

events. The family spirit of love and cooperation helped them all to think of ways they could bring in enough money to pay their bills. Soon they were renting out rooms of their large house to writers, scientists, professors, and students. The family never stopped studying music and singing together, and their boarders loved it.

One of the largest rooms was turned into a chapel, and a priest came to live with them to provide services for the students from the Catholic University. His name was Father Wasner. As a master musician, he began to train the family chorus, turning them from amateurs into professionals. Hence was born the "Trapp Family Singers," as the world would come to know them.

The learning and the singing became very serious now. The family practiced daily for six hours and more.

One evening, by chance, a great opera singer named Lotte Lehmann overheard the family singing in the garden.

"You must share your gift with the world. You cannot keep that music to yourselves. First you shall enter the festival for group singing. You can win easily, and others will have the opportunity to hear you," said Miss Lehmann enthusiastically.

"That we can't do. We couldn't sing for people from a stage," murmured Maria shyly.

"You be at that festival tomorrow. Your great gift must go out into the world," Miss Lehmann insisted.

"It isn't possible. We'd be too frightened," chimed in Johanna.

"I wouldn't care to see my family on a stage. It wouldn't be proper," the Captain joined in the protests.

But the next afternoon the "Trapp Family Singers," nervous and trembling, sang on the stage and won first prize! Perhaps it was as Lotte Lehmann had said: Theirs was a great talent and they should share it with the world. A radio appearance came next, and who should just happen to be listening?

None other than the Chancellor of the Austrian Republic, who promptly invited them to sing at a state reception. This performance was followed by a public concert and then a European tour. Everywhere the von Trapp Family sang, the people loved them.

On March 11, 1938, a strange-sounding voice came on the radio. It said, "Austria is dead. Long live the Third Reich!" Hitler had invaded Austria, and all of Europe was in the beginning of the Second World War.

Many things in the life of the von Trapp family changed. They did not sing anymore, for it was forbidden to sing the Austrian national anthem and Austrian folk songs. People could not say "hello" any more, only "Heil Hitler." All the names of streets and places in Salzburg were changed.

One day a member of the German police came to see the captain.

"You must remove the large Austrian flag that hangs in your hall. You must fly the swastika flag, the flag of the new Germany," he said.

"I'm sorry. We do not own a swastika flag. It costs much more than we can afford," replied the Captain.

"Then I shall be pleased to see that you have one," the officer answered, and he promptly brought a package from his car.

"I'm sorry," said the Captain again, "I cannot fly it for the colors are far too bright for this hall."

The officer left, displeased. For many days Maria feared that the police would be angry and take her husband away. It seemed a miracle to her when nothing happened.

Maria was then told that the teacher in school wanted to talk to her about the children.

"Your children refuse to sing our new anthem," said the teacher. "They tell me that their father says it will never be sung in his house. We have told the students they are the hope of our new nation and they are to disregard the old-fashioned ways of their parents. My advice to you is that you no longer discuss with your children what they learn in school now."

The von Trapp family could not bring themselves to do anything the new government was trying to force them to do. One day the teacher again called Maria to the school.

"Your children," she said severely, "will not practice our new greeting, 'Heil Hitler.' They simply refuse. If they continue, I shall have no choice but to report it to the police."

Shortly afterwards, the Captain received a letter from the government stating he should take command of a submarine in the Navy Department. This letter was followed by an order for the Trapp Family Singers to sing for Adolf Hitler's birthday.

The Captain called a solemn meeting of the family and told them it was

time to make a choice. Did they want the safety and comfort they could have if they stayed in Austria and worked for the new government? Or did they want their faith, honor, and freedom? He told them it was no longer possible to have both. As for himself, he would rather be poor and keep the spiritual things that meant more to him than life itself.

No one in the family hesitated. They began to make a very brave plan. They decided to leave their homeland and go to America. Leaving their house with everything in it, they took only a few things they could carry.

They pretended to be going on a skiing trip in the mountains, but they simply kept on going and were soon in Italy. A few days after they arrived there, the border was sealed by the Germans. After that no one was allowed to leave Austria.

When they arrived in America, everything was very strange. New York City was big and noisy! The buildings were so tall! In Vienna, the largest city in Austria, the tallest building was, at the most, six stories. When the von Trapp family was taken to their rooms on the nineteenth floor, they were all afraid they would somehow fall off!

The New York subway reminded the family of a fierce, underground dragon that roared, trembled, and perhaps ate passengers. In a large department store Maria was so frightened of the "moving stairs," the escalators, that she became rooted to the spot and would not step on. A large crowd of people gathered around to give her instructions and encouragement, but that only made her more embarrassed. Finally, she took a deep breath, closed her eyes, and put out her foot. She discovered the stair took her right along and even slid her off the top! What a strange country, America!

Here there were no frightening men in strange uniforms telling them what they could or could not do and say. The policemen the family met were kind and helpful. They could see that these people were new to America and did not yet understand American ways or speech. Everywhere they went they found people wanting to help them. It had been a difficult

journey from Austria to America, dangerous and frightening. The family was now very poor. All their money and their beautiful estate were gone. Only their family spirit, everyone working together and loving each other, had given them the courage to sacrifice for their beliefs.

They made a singing tour of America, but it was not a success. Somehow the kind of music they sang was not what Americans wanted to pay money to hear. Whenever a manager quit, they would sing for other managers, hoping one would hire them. But they all said the same thing: "American audiences won't pay to hear you. Your music is too strange, and you don't look very attractive." They wore the clothes they had brought with them from Austria. As for their program, they followed the suggestion given to them and added English and American songs. They wanted to sing for all kinds of people.

At last the family found a manager who agreed to hire them for one year.

"I will need five thousand dollars for all the advertising, for telling the people about you, and to get them to come to hear you," he told them.

"But we have exactly $250 in the bank!" gasped Maria.

"What you need is a miracle," said the manager.

"This family has never been short of miracles," replied Maria. "We will try."

The family had already made many friends in America, and soon several of their new friends offered to lend them the money they needed.

"You see," said Maria, "when God closes a door, somewhere he opens a window!" Family spirit and faith worked closely together for the von Trapp family.

It was four months until the next tour, and they had only fifty dollars to live on until then. They decided to have a "Trapp Family Handicraft Exhibit" and sell things they had made. They sold children's furniture, objects made of wood or clay, jewelry, leather—a whole collection of lovely folk art items.

And what do you suppose happened? Well, they sold everything so fast, they had to do another exhibit! The money they made lasted them until it was time for the tour. With their family spirit to help them, they always did whatever had to be done.

There were several concerts before the big tour. After each one their manager would say, "There's still something not quite right with your program. I can't tell exactly what it is, but I think you'll know what to do one of these times."

"What could it be," wondered Maria. "We've tried to do everything we possibly could do to please our audiences." The family talked about it often, trying to discover the secret they were lacking.

Then it happened. During a concert as Maria was yodeling (that is singing a fast, high mountain call from the Austrian Alps), she swallowed a fly! When the number was over, she felt she should explain her strange behavior to the audience, so she stepped forward and talked informally with them, making some funny remarks. Suddenly the audience was laughing and

feeling like it was one big, happy family. So that was the secret! The family no longer stood stiffly and solemnly on the stage, only interested in singing their music well. They talked with the audience and explained interesting things about their music. Everyone laughed together until the audience felt as if it had joined a musical party in the family living room.

The von Trapp family spirit had always included sharing their music with each other. Now they had found a way to share their gift with the people who paid to hear them sing, and they came to be greatly loved by their audiences. Their tours were now a huge success, and they went back and forth across the United States many times. Two sisters and a brother had been born into the family over the years and now, with Father Wasner, their group had grown to thirteen people. It was very hard work, staying each night in a different hotel, taking long rides on buses and trains, and singing hundreds of concerts.

Soon the von Trapp family was to know even more about work, for they found a farm they liked in the green hills of Vermont. It reminded them so much of Austria that they bought it and set about building their own house. This was especially hard, for the two boys were away in the Army. In addition to building a house, on the farm there would be pigs, sheep, cows, a garden, bees, an orchard, horses, machinery, and hay to look after. What a family spirit for work this von Trapp family had!

On the farm there was one particularly high hill. Maria loved to climb to the top. From there she could see many ranges of mountains and three valleys. She had been climbing mountains all her life, and they were like dear friends to her. She would think of the beautiful Austria she had left, and how it had been torn and crushed in the war. She knew it was by the will of God that she and her family had been led safely to America, where their singing could help lift the spirits and calm the fears of a people fighting a dreadful war.

"A part of your heart always remains behind in the land where you were born," she would say. "But now the family has come to love America."

Then came a sad time for the von Trapp family. The Captain became very ill. When he died, he was buried on Maria's hill, and thereafter this lone grave became a holy spot for the family.

The children began to marry and start families of their own. Those still able to do so joined with Maria and went singing, this time to many places around the world. The large house had many empty rooms now, so Maria turned it into a lodge where guests could come to stay and enjoy beautiful Vermont. The Trapp Family Music Camp brought people from all over the world to spend ten days at a time with the family learning how to bring music into the lives of their own families. Maria's ideas and her way of loving and serving people went on and on. She began to give lectures in many places, telling about her family with warmth and humor. Over and over she repeated her special message: "Each of us must find out the will of God and go and do it. Let us love one another as God has loved us."

Now I have told you the story of a family whose spirit became great because they had two special things they shared with each other and the world—their music and their love. Could your family find its own special note to bring to this world? Maria would surely say, "Yes!"